- Heidi Splete

101 Marathon Tips

LifeTips Book Series

By Heidi Splete
Marathon Expert Guru
LifeTips

LifeTips
Move Up In Life.
LifeTips Book Series
Boston, Massachusetts

LIFETIPS PRESIDENT: Byron White

BOOK SERIES EDITOR: Melanie Nayer

All inquires should be addressed to:

LifeTips.com, Inc.
101 Book Series
One First Avenue
Building 34, Suite 200
Charlestown, MA 02129
(617) 886-9001
http://www.LifeTips.com

International Standard Book No. 978-1-60275-016-6

Table of Contents

A Note from the Editor

Whether you're a novice runner or a marathon champ, knowing the tricks and tips of running – no matter what distance – is essential. Not only do you improve your time and meet your physical goals, but the proper training and guidance helps prevent injuries.

I'm currently training for my first marathon and I can say this – it's not easy. But Heidi's tips have helped me put things in perspective. Everything from setting realistic training goals to the right type of socks is important when you're running a marathon, and Heidi covers it all in this book.

The most important lesson: listen to your body. Heidi talks about this throughout her book and offers ways to stay in tune with your body as you're approaching the 26 mile marker. It's an incredible accomplishment!

While Heidi's tips will come in handy as I continue to train for my marathon, I am certainly looking forward to Heidi's post-marathon tip: get a massage!

Melanie Nayer
Editor, LifeTips.com

A Note from the Author

I've conquered everything from the 5K to 50K, but the marathon is my favorite. The 26.2-mile distance is a test of endurance, consistency, and mental toughness rather than speed. Whether you are training for your first marathon or your fiftieth, I hope this book provides unique insight and inspiration that you can use and adapt during your marathon training and running in general.

My ongoing goal is to educate, encourage, and entertain runners and potential runners. For more of my running, health, and fitness tips, visit lifetips.com.

Heidi Splete is a seasoned marathon runner and a health, fitness, and medical writer. She started running on the cross-country and track teams in junior high school, and continued to compete in both sports throughout high school and college. She ran her first marathon in 1992 and got hooked on the 26.2-mile distance. Her total number of marathons completed is approaching 30, and her running resume includes several big-city marathons, including the Boston Marathon, Marine Corps Marathon, New York City Marathon, and Honolulu Marathon.

Keeping running!

Heidi Splete
LifeTips Expert Guru

1| Build Mileage Gradually

Whether you are a beginning runner or a beginning marathoner, build mileage gradually when training for a marathon to let your body adapt to running longer distances. If you are new to running and you want to train for a marathon, give yourself several months of training time so you can build mileage and endurance. Don't increase your weekly mileage by more than 10 percent per week and you'll reduce your risk of overuse injuries. *Runner's World* magazine, either in print or online at runnersworld.com, is a great resource that includes detailed suggestions for beginning runners. Some of these plans include timed periods of walking during long training runs, and some beginning marathoners find that a combination of walking and running a useful way to build strength and confidence as they cover longer distances, especially those who are new to running, not just to marathoning. Some runners, both beginning and experienced, follow a walk-run plan to complete the marathon, but even beginners can run the entire distance successfully if you give yourself time to build mileage and if you cross train to build strength and endurance.

2| Check Out Your Local Running Club

If you are new to marathons, you may find it helpful to run longer distances with one or two friends or with a larger group for safety as well as for socializing. Seek out running clubs in your area to find company for your weekly long runs. Not only do some of these groups arrange to place water in strategic locations, but they will know where you can safely run 15-20 miles. If you prefer to run by yourself, use the local club as a resource to help you plot a route for a long run if you aren't sure where to go. Also, many local running clubs can recommend local sports medicine professionals, such as podiatrists and chiropractors, who are sympathetic to runners.

3| Asphalt Over Cement

Many beginning runners think that running on a cement sidewalk is no different from running on an asphalt road. Not so. Asphalt has some "give," while cement has none. If you regularly run on cement sidewalks, you may find that your feet or lower legs start to hurt as you increase your mileage. Try to run in neighborhoods or on side roads where you can run on the street rather than the sidewalk, and seek out asphalt paths wherever possible. When you run on any road or street, be sure to run on the left, facing traffic, and stay on or near the shoulder of the road.

4| If You Hurt, Get Help

It almost goes without saying, but if you experience any type of pain beyond the next-day soreness of a tough workout, if any muscles are visibly bruised, swollen, or warm, or if something just doesn't feel right, visit a sports medicine professional. Experienced runners know that it is better to catch an injury early, identify the cause, and solve the problem then to keep running with chronic pain. There's no point in being stubborn and allowing something to get worse and sidetrack your training. The majority of running injuries are easy to correct and you can prevent them from recurring. Don't be afraid to go to a podiatrist, orthopedist, or other sports medicine professional. The right person will not say, "Just stop running." He or she will help you keep running, or modify your workouts until you heal.

- If your feet are bothering you, start with a podiatrist. Ask runners you know or check with a local running store or club to find someone who treats runners.
- If your knees, hips, or back are the problem, try an orthopedist or a sports medicine specialist.
- Some people have great success with chiropractors for help in managing minor knee, hip, and foot problems. Make sure you get a recommendation from a friend or colleague, fellow runner, or another sports medicine professional.

5| Listen To Your Body, Learn Your Pace

As you start running longer distances to train for a marathon, pay attention to your muscles, your feet, and how your body responds in different temperatures, and after different distances. When you increase your mileage, decrease your pace so you can run the entire distance at approximately the same speed. If you are used to sprinting for 3 miles for a workout, you will need to moderate your pace as you adjust to a longer distance. Your easy runs should be easy enough for you to carry on a conversation with your fellow runners. Not only does a "conversational pace" ensure that you aren't going too fast, it makes the run more fun.

6| Post-Marathon: Let Yourself Recover

It takes your body a few weeks to recover from a marathon, especially for beginners. Even though you feel great, resist the temptation to sign up for that other marathon in town three weeks later. You can get away with this once you have had some experience with marathons and your body is used to the stress, but it is always a risk because you are still recovering. Even if you didn't run hard or fast, be sure to respect the marathon distance, because your body will respond with an overuse injury if you don't allow time to rest. But rest doesn't mean that you have to sit and do nothing (although that's fine, too). Walking is a great post-marathon activity, as is easy running, biking, and yoga. I'm not saying don't run, but give yourself at least few weeks off from weekly long runs if you want to train for another marathon.

7| Stay Motivated By Enjoying The Journey

Some beginning marathoners are motivated by a cause and they are running and raising money for a charity. Others simply see it as a personal challenge. Regardless of your reason for running a marathon, staying motivated during long runs can be hard, especially if its cold, or raining, or if you have had a long week. If you like to listen to music, bring your favorite tunes, with you, but please don't tune out your surroundings; you still need to watch for traffic or other hazards when running. Running with a group or even one training partner also boosts motivation, and talking to fellow runners helps the miles go by remarkably quickly. Or, use the time to clear your head and review issues from your work or personal life and think about pleasant events to come, such as your non-running weekend plans or your next vacation. Remind yourself (as often as necessary) that you will enjoy the experience and look forward to the accomplishment of completing a marathon.

8| Don't Train For Short And Long Distances At The Same Time

Keep in mind that it is hard to train simultaneously for a marathon and for a 10K, or another short race. If you are doing high-intensity speed workouts and weekly long training runs, you are at increased risk of injury because these are two different types of running but both are stressful to your muscles. Focus on one race at a time. A speed workout in a marathon training plan usually involves longer intervals (such as an 8-minute tempo run, or mile intervals), while a runner focusing on a 5K or 10K will want to do shorter intervals, such as 200- or 400-meter repeats. If you are using the 10K itself as a tempo run that is incorporated into your marathon training plan, you don't need to obsess about doing a lot of 200- or 400-meter intervals to prepare for that 10K. Save your competitive 10K training for when you are not also training for a marathon.

9| Half Marathons Help You Hone Your Marathon Pacing

Half-marathons (13.1 miles) are a great way to help you get a sense of what your marathon pace may be. If you are really pushing yourself in a half marathon you will probably be running faster than you would for a full marathon. But if you run a half marathon at a pace that is slightly faster than your usual pace for long, slow distance runs (too fast to talk easily, but not so fast that you are exhausted), you will develop a sense of how it feels to maintain a consistent, but slightly faster pace for 13.1 miles. Ideally, when you finish a half marathon that you are using as a training run, you should feel like you could run the course again at a similar pace and feel tired but not completely wiped out.

10| Include Pre-Race Warm-up Prior To A Short Race

If you are running a short distance race of 10 miles or less, warm up with a 10-minute warm-up jog, especially if you plan to run faster than a normal training run. A warm-up jog is just that—slow and easy running. But remember to time yourself and don't run too far away from the start. You don't want to find yourself sprinting back to the starting line at the last minute.

11| Short Distance Recovery Runs: Keep Them Short

When a marathon training plan calls for a short run, it is usually less than 8 miles. Even if you feel great, resist the urge to add mileage. The weekly long training run is the important mileage builder in marathon training, and short runs on the other days of the week are part of the recovery process. You won't be any less conditioned if you run 5 miles rather than 10 miles on a random Wednesday when you are running 17 miles on Saturday.

12| Use Short Intervals To Train For Short Distances

If you aren't running a marathon anytime soon and your current goal is to run a great 10K in two months, try some speed work. If you don't have access to a track, or if you do but you prefer not to run around in circles, try this workout once a week: Start with your favorite 8-10 mile run. Use your watch and run at a normal pace for 8-10 minutes, then pick up the pace to about 80 percent of your maximum effort (not a full-out sprint, but too fast to talk) for 2 minutes, then drop back to an easy, relaxed pace for 2 minutes. Then pick up the pace for 4 minutes, run easy for 2 minutes, pick up the pace for 6 minutes, run easy for 2 minutes, pick up the pace for 8 minutes, run easy for 2 minutes, then reverse the process and pick up the pace for 6 minutes, then run easy for 2 minutes, pick up the pace for 4 minutes run easy for 2 minutes, pick up the pace for 2 minutes, then run easy for 2 minutes. Give yourself at least 5 minutes of easy running at the end of the workout, and you may run for an easy 15-20 minutes at the end of the workout if you are on a 10-mile route. You can both stop and start your watch for each pickup time or let it go continuously; these times don't have to be exact to the second.

13| Use Short Races As Tempo Runs

A 5K, 10K, or 10-mile race is a great way to work some speed into your marathon training if you don't like (or don't choose) to do tempo runs or interval workouts. But remember that the pace you run for these races, especially for a 5K, will probably not be the pace you will maintain during a marathon, and that's OK. Running faster than your likely marathon pace will build strength and endurance, and running fast in short races will ultimately make you faster over the long distances, too, just as speed work on a track or tempo runs on the road make you faster.

14| Use Short Races To Test Gear And Strategies

Short races can be a great way test a new brand of socks, shorts, or any other gear that you might use in a marathon to see how it works in a race situation. Avoid wearing or using anything brand-new in any race; try to test something on a training run first. But it can be reassuring to see how certain plans work in a race situation, such as whether you can easily carry two packs of gel in your new shorts (even if you are not eating any of them during a 10K race) and whether you can throw away an extra shirt at a water stop on a chilly day without getting tangled up in it.

15| You Don't Need Speedy Shoes For Short Distance Races

Some runners who are serious competitors in 5-K and 10-K races wear heavier shoes for long runs and marathons and change to their "performance trainers" for shorter races. I only recommend this if you are an experienced runner without any major biomechanical problems. Unless you are a top-level competitor, you aren't going to get an edge from wearing thinner, lighter shoes, especially if you are running on the road rather than on a track. If you wear shoes with insufficient support and cushioning for a 10-K race, your feet and knees will let you know, and you probably won't make that mistake again.

16| All Mileage Is Not Created Equal

Many runners enjoy running on trails, and trail running can provide relief from the road's asphalt or cement. But running the same distance on a trail will take longer than it will on the road, and you'll be working harder to maintain your footing. Some trail running requires a combination of running and hiking depending on the difficulty of the terrain. If trail running appeals to you, it won't hurt your preparation for a marathon, but be prepared to walk or climb over rough spots and allow more time to complete the run. A 6 mile trail run may leave you more tired than a 10-mile run on the road. You can run on most trails in any running shoes without a problem. But if you plan to do a lot of trail running, especially on uneven or hilly trails, consider investing in a pair of trail running shoes for the additional traction that these shoes provide. But wear your standard training shoes for road runs. Running on the road will wear out the tread of your trail shoes and destroy the benefit of that extra traction.

17| Core Body Strength: Abs and Back

The "core body" refers to the muscles of your torso that help you maintain your posture, whether you are running, standing, or sitting. Strong abdominal and lower back muscles will combat fatigue during the marathon and during long training runs. Sit-ups, in any form, are among the easiest and most effective ways to strengthen the abdominal muscles, but you can use an abdominal machine at the gym, too. Although most runners exercise their abdominal muscles, they often neglect the back. Most of us harbor some tension in the lower back because of time spent sitting at a desk. Try this exercise to release some of that tension: Lie on your back with your knees bent and feet flat on the floor, and your arms by your sides. Tighten your gluteal (butt) muscles and abdominal muscles simultaneously and flatten your lower back onto the floor. Hold for a count of 5, then relax, and repeat 2-3 times.

18| Get On The Ball

Fitness balls will help strengthen your core muscles, and they are fun to use. Simply sitting on a fitness ball while watching TV engages your abdominal and lower back muscles as they work to keep you from falling off the ball. But you'll reap greater benefits with some basic ball exercises. Here's my favorite: the basic fitness ball sit-up: Start by sitting on the ball and roll back so the ball is centered under your shoulder blades and your head is dropped back towards the floor behind you. Place your hands on your ears and curl up into a sit-up. Release. Start by repeating 10 times and work up to 30. If you are new to fitness balls, keep your legs wide (3-4 feet) as you sit on the ball. Once that feels easy, move your feet closer together so they are shoulder-width apart; this makes the sit-up more challenging.

19| Lift Weights To Prevent Injury By Balancing Your Muscles

A moderate weightlifting program helps marathoners strengthen muscles that aren't used in running. If running is your only form of exercise, certain muscles, such as the hamstrings, will become stronger, but the quadricep muscles will not. This imbalance can set the stage for an injury. When you are working out with weights, try to use the same or similar amounts of weight for opposing muscle groups, such as the biceps and triceps, or the quads and hamstrings. The weights you are lifting with your hamstrings may feel easy, but that's OK. Your hamstrings get plenty of exercise from running. If the amount of weight you need to challenge your hamstrings is a struggle for your quads, it is better to lift less weight with the hamstrings than to overtax your quads. Once you build more strength in your quads, you will fell comfortable lifting the same amount of weight with both muscle groups. You don't need to spend hours in the gym for effective weight training. In half an hour, you can fit in 2-3 sets of 10-15 repetitions for a few key muscle groups:

- hamstrings/quadriceps
- adductor/abductor muscles (inner and outer hip)
- the calf muscles
- biceps/triceps
- shoulders

The weight should be heavy enough that your muscles start to feel tired during the second or third set.

20| Pool Running: An Injured Runner's Best Friend

If you are injured or recovering from almost any type of injury, running in a pool is a wonderful cross-training activity. You can wear a specially designed belt that allows you to move your arms and legs just as if you were running on land. Or, if you don't have a belt, you can use a kickboard. Place the kickboard under your chest and wrap your arms under it. Your feet will hang down into the water. Use a normal running motion to propel yourself forward. The kickboard version of pool running is less aerobic than using a belt, but you will still work your leg muscles.

21| Stationary Biking Builds Leg Strength With Less Stress

If you can't run because of an injury or bad weather, riding a stationary bike is a cross-training option that is available at most gyms. Biking is a good alternative to running if you have a foot injury because you aren't putting much pressure on your feet. Biking is also a safe alternative exercise for some knee and hip injuries, as well. Even if you aren't injured, biking is a great supplemental activity to running because you can pedal at a brisk pace and build leg strength without the additional pressure on your joints. You can design your own tempo workout on a bike by pedaling at about 80% of your maximum effort for 2 minutes, then easy for 2 minutes, and repeat several times. Steady pedaling will build length strength, too. Spinning is a different type of cross training on a bike that involves high-speed pedaling and it is a more intense workout than steady biking. If you take part in a spinning class, your legs will be as tired as they would be if you did speed work on a track. If that appeals to you, try it, but be ready to sweat. Before you start any type of biking, be sure to adjust the seat. The right seat height feels comfortable, and you should not be straining to reach the pedals. Your knees should not bend more than a 90-degree angle while you are pedaling, and you should have a slight bend in your knee when your leg is extended. If the seat is set incorrectly, you could set yourself up for an injury because you are stressing your legs in an unnatural position.

22| Treadmill Running: An Indoor Alternative

If you can't (or prefer not to) run outside, you can train for a marathon on a treadmill. Note: this is not recommend for long training runs of 10 miles or more (although runners do run that far on treadmills). Treadmills offer a more forgiving surface than asphalt or concrete, and some runners find them a pleasant change from harder surfaces, and a more appealing option in the winter. But treadmill running does take some getting used to; be careful when starting and stopping your run so you don't fall, and make sure that your shoelaces are not dragging. And if you notice any leg or foot pain after a few treadmill runs, go back outside or try a different treadmill. A cheap model may not have a surface that feels good after 5-6 miles of running. Want a hill workout? Most treadmills can be adjusted to various degrees of incline to make the run more challenging.

23| Twice Weekly Weights Work Well For Marathoners

Try to do some type of strength training twice weekly, with at least one day off between weight training sessions. You'll not only get stronger, you will be able to run longer and faster. As long as you keep the weights at a moderately challenging amount, you are not in danger of bulking up to body-builder proportions. If you already lift weights, stick with your normal routine and it will help your marathon training, but don't schedule a weight training session on the day before or the day after a long training run. If you lift on the day before a long run, you may be unnecessarily tired, and if you lift the day after a long run, you will be tired and at greater risk for pulling a muscle while you are lifting. If you are new to weight training, ask someone at your local gym to show you the correct way to use the machines and free weights that are available. You don't need to do more than one or two exercises for each of the main muscle groups, so try a few different machines and decide which you like best for each muscle group.

24| Walking Helps You Recover From Running

Don't underestimate walking as a cross-training tool. Walking is gentler on your joints than running, but it still works your muscles and promotes circulation in the legs and feet. Walking can help you maintain a basic level of fitness if an injury keeps you from running. I think of walking as a restorative activity; if my legs feel sore after a long run, I have found that a one-mile (or 20-30 minute) walk later that day or the next day helps relieve the stiffness and soreness.

25| Yoga Combats Runners' Stiffness

Running has many benefits, but increased flexibility is not among them. If you have access to a gym or yoga studio that offers yoga classes, make an effort to find a beginner class and fit it into your schedule. Even one class a week will make a difference in your strength and flexibility. I have been attending a yoga class once or twice a week for about 10 years, and my marathon times have improved. Coincidence? I think not. Any type of yoga class (Ashtanga, Bikram, or Hatha) encourages you to stretch more deeply than most of us do on our own. Yoga also works muscles that you don't use in running, which promotes muscle balance and reduces your risk of injury. Yoga makes you stronger, too. It isn't a substitute for weight training, but you will build upper-body strength without bulking up. You'll be forced to work on your core muscles of your abdominal and back muscles by holding your body in the yoga poses. And an Ashtanga-style or "power yoga" class provides an aerobic workout, too.

26| Arm Circles Help Your Shoulders Relax

The muscles in the upper back often become tense while running, especially when running long distances. You can reduce this tension by adding arm circles to your stretching routine.

- Stand with your arms pointing straight out to either side.
- Use both arms simultaneously and make 10 circles in one direction, then 10 circles in the other direction.

This simple exercise does help to relieve tension in the upper back, which can be especially tight for people who, when they are not training for a marathon, spend much of their time working at a computer.

27| Calf Stretching: No Bull

If you only do one running-related exercise, make it a calf stretch. Several common running injuries, including plantar fasciitis and Achilles tendonitis, are exacerbated (if not caused) by tight calf muscles. My favorite calf stretch is the "wall push."

- Place your forearms or hands against a wall.
- Bend one leg and place the foot of the bent leg flat on the floor.
- Step the other leg straight back, place the back foot flat on the floor, and keep both feet pointing straight ahead.
- Concentrate on bringing your hips towards the wall, while keeping your back foot flat on the floor.
- You should feel a stretch in the calf of the back leg. Hold an easy stretch for a count of 30.
- Don't bounce. If you bounce, you could strain your calf rather than stretch it.
- For a slightly deeper stretch, raise the foot of your bent leg of the floor for a few seconds and place it back on the floor while you are counting to 30.

But wait, there's more. Before you switch to the opposite leg, bend the knee of the back leg and hold in an easy stretch for about 5 seconds. This move will stretch the soleus muscle, which is a muscle in the upper calf. Now you can repeat the stretch for the other leg.

28| Don't Forget Your Upper Body

Runners naturally focus on their legs and feet, but running tightens the muscles of the arms, back, and shoulders, too. Don't neglect these muscles. You want to have a full range of motion in your arms when running a marathon because even if you don't realize it, your upper body strength will help keep you going when you're tired. Try this simple triceps stretch.

- Reach your right arm overhead and then bend it at the elbow so your right hand reaches down towards your shoulder blades.
- Reach up and grasp your right elbow with your left hand and gently pull your elbow down, creating a stretch in your triceps and upper shoulder.
- Don't pull hard on your elbow; this is a gentle stretch.
- Hold it while you count to 15.
- Release your arms and repeat on the other side.

29| Extreme Elevation: Legs Up Against The Wall

Elevation of an injured area is an important principle of first aid, but elevating your legs regularly is a restorative exercise for anyone and for marathoners in particular because we ask so much of our legs and feet. One of my high school running coaches told us to elevate our feet after practices now and then, and one of my yoga teachers periodically suggests that we place our legs against the wall for a few minutes at the end of the class. Here's how you do it:

- Find a door or an empty patch of wall space. Lie on a blanket or towel if you are on a hard floor.
- Lie flat on your back, and then lift your legs and rest your feet on the wall. If you can, scoot as close to the wall as possible so that your legs touch the wall, too, and the base of your lower back is 2-3 inches from the wall.
- Stay in this position for at least 2-3 minutes, or as long as 10 minutes.

This simple exercise revitalizes your legs, and you should notice a feeling of lightness, especially if you can stay in the position for at least 5 minutes.

30| Getting Hip: Hip Stretches

Hip stretches are difficult for many runners because distance running promotes tight hips. You may not notice when your hips are tight, but you will notice when they are loose; you'll feel that your running stride is easier and more relaxed if you do some hip stretches. Hip stretches are especially helpful after a run, but do them before you run if that is more convenient, or do them in any spare moment.

- Sit on the floor with the left knee bent and left foot flat on the floor.
- Bend the right leg and place the right foot on top of the left knee; your right knee should point out to the right side.
- Support yourself with your hands so you don't fall backwards. You should feel a stretch in the outer part of your hip.
- Hold for a count of 10, then switch legs and repeat on the other side.

31| Give The IT Band A Hand

The iliotibial band, also known as the IT band, is a thick band of tissue that runs along the outside of each leg. The IT band helps keep the legs and knees stable as they move, and if it becomes inflamed or irritated, it can cause pain in the knees, hips, or outer thighs. A tight IT band is more vulnerable to irritation, and running long distances tends to make it tight. Keep your IT band happy with this stretch:

- Stand up straight and cross one foot over the other.
- Bend forward from the hips and reach your hands towards the floor.
- Keep your feet flat on the floor and don't move them, but engage your leg muscles as if you were trying to move your feet closer to each other. This action should engage the IT band along the outside of the back leg.
- Hold for a count of 10, then relax, and engage the muscles again.
- Stand up, cross the opposite leg over, and repeat on the other side.

32| Protect Your Knees When Stretching Your Quads

To gently stretch your quadriceps (the large muscles of the thighs) and protect your knees, try a standing quad stretch.

- Start by standing on the right foot and bending your left knee.
- Reach back and grasp your *left* foot with your *right* hand. This technique keeps the knee bent at a more natural angle than if you grasp the left foot with the left hand, and you protect the knee from excessive stress.
- Hold the stretch comfortably and count to 30.
- Be sure to stand next to a wall or sturdy table, chair, or railing that you can hold for balance.

Strong quads are important for marathon runners because the quads support the knees and keep them stable, especially when running downhill.

33| Stretching: Try It, You'll Like It

Although findings from several sports medicine studies in recent years suggest that people who stretch are not significantly less likely to suffer sports injuries compared with people who don't stretch, my experience suggests that stretching doesn't hurt, it won't increase your risk of injury, and it feels good. You don't have to spend a lot of time stretching. A 5-10 minute stretching routine that includes stretching your calves, hips, quads, and hamstrings before you run can make for a more comfortable run. Most runners recognize the benefits of some stretching as a way to release muscle tension prior to a workout. If you are stressed or tired or nervous before a run or a race, your muscles will be tense, and tense muscles are more easily injured than relaxed muscles. Your primary goal in stretching should be to release tension, and increasing your flexibility will be a positive side effect. Some principles of stretching:

- Never stretch to the point of pain. When you feel a stretch in a muscle, stop and hold it at that point.
- Stretching is not a competitive sport and trying to stretch as far as the person next to you will only leave you with a pulled muscle and a sense of frustration.
- Remember to breathe normally. Don't hold your breath while stretching.

34| The Butterfly Stretch Relaxes The Groin

Nobody wants to suffer a groin pull, especially not a runner who is training for a marathon, because these injuries can take a long time to heal. Consistent but gentle stretching may reduce your chances of injury, and a simple butterfly stretch is part of my pre-run routine.

- Sit on the floor and place the soles of your feet together.
- Keep your feet as close to your body as possible.
- If your hips are tight, your knees will be high; if you have flexible hips, your knees may come close to the floor.
- Hold your ankles and bend forward from the waist.
- Place your elbow against your inner thighs and push down gently as you bend forward to help move your knees toward the floor.
- **Remember**: Do NOT stretch to the point of pain.

35| Treat Your Feet To A Tennis Ball Roll

Rolling your foot across the top of a tennis ball is almost as good as a foot massage and it serves the same purpose of increasing the circulation and working out tight muscles in your feet. When you roll your foot over a tennis ball, you stretch the muscles on the bottoms of your feet, which can help prevent plantar fasciitis. And it feels good! For best results, stand up. You can do this exercise while seated, but you will be able to exert more direct pressure if you stand.

- Place a tennis ball on the floor.
- Hold onto a chair, table, or wall for support.
- Place your foot on top of the ball and roll the ball up and down the length of your foot and from side to side. Don't worry if you feel some cracking or popping in the joints of your foot. That is normal, especially if you often wear tight-fitting shoes.
- Roll your foot around on the ball for a minute or two, and then repeat the exercise with the other foot.

You can do this as often as you want, anytime your feet feel tired or tight.

36| Use Props To Help Stretch Tight Hamstrings

Runners tend to develop tight hamstrings (the large muscles on the backs of the legs) because these muscles do much of the work in distance running. There are many ways to stretch the hamstrings, but you only need to do one or two exercises during any single stretching routine. Try this hamstring exercise for a good hamstring stretch.

- Start standing up and place the heel of one foot on a bench, chair, or table, at a height that lets you comfortably keep the raised leg straight. If you feel a strain, place your foot on something lower.
- Keep your standing leg fairly straight, but don't lock your knee.
- Keep your standing foot pointing straight ahead in a normal running or walking position.
- Look straight ahead and slowly bend forward from the waist until you feel a stretch in the back of your thigh.
- Hold it for a count of 10, then relax, and try again. Remember:
- Don't bounce; stretch gently and relax. Repeat with the other leg.

If standing on one leg makes you uncomfortable, you can stretch your hamstrings while sitting on the floor.

- Start with one leg straight out in front of you.
- Bend your other knee and place your foot against the inner thigh of the straight leg; your bent knee will drop towards the floor.

37| Don't Be A Mileage Monger

When you start training for a marathon, give yourself at least 3 months to build up your mileage. Gradually building up mileage is the best way to avoid an overuse injury. As you build up your mileage, don't increase your weekly mileage total by more than 10 percent per week. If your goal is to finish the marathon feeling reasonably good, you probably don't need to run much more than 50 miles a week, total. Once you have reached 40-50 miles, which includes your weekday runs and your weekend long run, you can hold steady at that level of mileage and you will be able to complete the marathon, especially if you build strength with cross-training workouts such as biking, weight lifting, and yoga. Remember that your muscles get stronger during periods of rest, and not every week will be a high-mileage week, which is a good thing.

38| Don't Let Your Time Overtake You

Following a specific time puts pressure on you that you don't need, and it doesn't allow for variables. For example, you might have a slightly slower mile before you make that pit stop when nature calls, and you'll make up for it with a faster mile because you will feel better. Try to run the marathon at a steady but comfortable pace, and pick it up when you feel good, and try to hold the pace when you start to get tired. Rather than focusing on the fact that your last mile was 20 seconds slower than the mile before that, tell yourself, "I'm going to pick out a person ahead of me and pass them within this next mile." Don't sprint; instead focus on catching up to that person gradually, without exerting more than 80 percent of your maximum effort. Once you pass that person (which may take only 200 yards), pick someone else, and before you know it you will have picked up your pace slightly, but not so fast that you feel worn out.

39| Finding Your Consistent Pace

Your ideal marathon pace should be something that you can keep up consistently. My best marathons are those when my times for each mile have been within a minute of each other. Resist the urge to run the first mile too fast, although your adrenaline is pumping and you want to get off to a good start. When you pass the first mile, that is one of the few times you can check your watch. If you usually train at an 8:30 pace and you ran the first mile at 6:47, you need to relax immediately. After that, stop checking your watch at every mile. Once you have passed the first mile and adjusted your pace if necessary, find a rhythm that is a little faster than your training runs, (too fast to comfortably carry on a conversation, but not so fast that you are wearing yourself out). Some miles will be slower than others, but that's OK. And it's OK to talk to people, too, especially if you are running with a friend. Sometimes it's more important (and more fun) to keep each other going and talk than to pick up the pace and not talk. On the flip side, don't panic if your first mile is as much as 2-3 minutes slower than your training pace because you are caught in the crowd of 20,000 people at the start. Starting slow conserves your energy and helps you loosen up. You have 26.2 miles to make up a few minutes if you need to.

40| Great Expectations: Three Marathon Goals

There are three layers of goals in running a marathon. The first goal is to finish, and if you train smart, you should be able to accomplish that. The second goal is to finish feeling (relatively) good. If you train well and take care of yourself, and pace yourself during the marathon, you should finish on your feet and uninjured. You might be exhausted and wondering, "Has anyone seen a finish line around here?" during the last few miles, but that is different from staggering across the finish line in pain because you ran too fast for the first 10 miles. The third goal is your finishing time. Many marathoners have a Boston Marathon qualifying time as their goal, and that's fine, but beginners in particular should not fixate on a specific time. And don't fixate on those time charts that project what your marathon time will be based on 5K and 10K times; the marathon is a unique race, and a lot can happen in 26.2 miles. Pick an approximate time that you think you can manage, such as "under 5 hours," or "under 4 hours" and remember that if you don't meet that goal, your primary goal was to finish.

41| Hill Running: Just Do It, But Watch Your Quads

Running up and down hills will certainly make you stronger. Some runners do "hill repeats" by finding a hill and running up and down several times. The potential problem with hill repeats is that running downhill takes a toll on the quadriceps muscles, which are often weak in distance runners who don't make the effort to strengthen them with cross-training exercises. You don't need to run hill repeats to reap the benefits, though. Finding a long training run that includes some rolling hills, if possible. Not every long run has to be hilly, but even if you can do a hilly long run once or twice during your marathon training, you will get the endurance benefits of a long run and the strength building benefits of hills. Don't run up and down the stairs. This type of running is jarring to the knees, and you are more likely to trip on stairs than you are to trip on a sloping street.

42| Mind Games: The Mental Side Of Marathons

Running a marathon is an intense physical activity, no doubt about it. But successful marathoners recognize that there is a mental side, too. Knowing that you are well prepared for the marathon will boost your confidence. That preparation comes from training. During your training you have learned that you can complete long runs and run again the next day, you have learned what flavor of energy gel you like best, and you have learned that good quality socks are worth the money. Also, and it sounds clichè, but a positive attitude is an asset during a marathon. If you find yourself slowing down or stopping to walk because it is 85 degrees, or you went out too fast, or you tried that weird gel at mile 15, tell yourself that your first goal is to finish, and you can almost always do that, unless you are truly ill or injured. Most athletes, and runners are no exception, tend to be superstitious, and if you have your "lucky training socks" or your "racing bandana" that no one else knows about, it's normal. Just don't let superstition paralyze you and keep you from feeling good about the marathon if something goes awry. If the dog hid your "lucky socks" the day before the race, that's why you have more than one pair on hand, and if you can't find chocolate gel, strawberry will be lucky, too.

43| Tempo Runs: Speed Without The Track

If you want to work some speed into your marathon training but you don't like running around a track or don't have access to one, try working some tempo runs into your distance runs. Check out the short distance section for an example of a more intense tempo run, but you can create a less regimented version. Here's how to do it:

- During any medium distance run during the week, simply pick a point on your route or a time on your watch, and pick up the pace for 5 minutes.
- Don't sprint; keep the pace at about 80 percent of your maximum effort.
- Then slow done and run at a relaxed pace for 10 minutes, then do another 5-minute pickup.

Not wearing a watch? Pick up the pace until you reach the end of the street. Create your own tempo runs; pick up the pace for 3 minutes, or 10 minutes, or even 20 minutes, during the middle of a weekday run. But when the schedule calls for an easy run, keep those runs easy. Tempo runs are the equivalent of a track workout or hill workout.

44| The Need For Speed: It's Your Choice

Many marathon training plans call for speed workouts as a way to build strength. That's fine, and you may run a faster marathon if you do speed work as part of your training, but the strength you build by cross training delivers similar benefits if tempo runs or intervals don't appeal to you. If your marathon goal is to finish, the most important thing you can do to train is simply to run, at a comfortable pace, most days a week, and to get that long run in once a week. If you enjoy running interval workouts on a track and you regularly do speed workouts with fellow runners, it won't hurt your marathon training, but don't do strenuous workouts two days in a row. Your muscles need time to recover. Some advanced marathon training plans call for more than one speed workout or tempo run per week. If you are following this type of plan, be sure to factor an easy day between the speed days. For example, do your speed workouts or hill workouts on Monday and Wednesday, or Tuesday and Thursday, and run some easy, short runs or cross-train on the alternate days. If you do a tempo run on Monday, run an easy 4-8 miles on Tuesday, and that's a good day to do some weight lifting. If you are doing one speed workout or hill workout in a week, try to do it on Tuesday or Wednesday so you have time to recover before your weekend long run.

45| The Power Of Rest: Don't Skip A Day Off

When I was a college student competing in track and cross-country running, I ran 7 days a week. I was lucky I didn't get injured, but your body can get away with more when you are 20 years old. When I started training for marathons after college, I researched some basic marathon training plans and all the ones I found recommended at least one rest day of no running. Some plans call for two rest days. Some runners like to take Sunday off after a long run on Saturday, others like to take a day off during the week when they need some extra time during the day for something else, or they make a spur-of-the moment decision to take a day off on a cold, rainy Tuesday. Rest doesn't mean lying on the sofa all day, although that's fine. You can bike, swim, chase your kids, or go shopping. Just don't run. Those muscles that you use in running will know that they aren't being used to run, and they will recover more effectively, even if you are engaged in some other activity.

46| Training Plans Are Made For Tweaking

Don’t become obsessed with your training plan. Your marathon will not be ruined if you didn’t run seven miles on Thursday because you were up all night with a sick child or if you were on a business trip. Training plans are made for adjustment. Use them as guides, and adapt them to suit yourself, your life, your goals, and unforeseen circumstances such as injuries or bad weather. As long as you can do a long run once a week during most weeks leading up to the marathon, you will be able to complete the race. If you want to do speed workouts and hill workouts, that’s great, just don’t worry if you miss a few. During the week, listen to your body and run mostly middle distances, from 5-8 miles, at a comfortable pace. Find a training plan that seems to suit your needs and goals and adapt it. If you want to do some speed work one week but not the next week, that's fine. There is no one plan that guarantees better results than any other plan. Check out runnersworld.com to give you some ideas for basic training plans depending on your goals.

47| Weekly Long Run: The Main Ingredient In Marathon Training

Want a recipe for marathon success? Be sure to include a long run once a week for 10-12 weeks. The length of that long run varies, but it's recommended that you two or three training runs of at least 20 miles during the few months before the marathon. The key is to stagger the weeks for the longest runs. Running 20 miles on two consecutive Saturdays is feasible, but it is not necessary and it is not the best way to train because your body doesn't have much time to recover. Assuming that you are running at least 20 miles a week for 5-8 miles at a time, start by running 8-10 miles one weekend. The next weekend, run 10-12 miles, and then next weekend, try for 12-15 miles, but the weekend after that, drop back to 10 miles. Then run 15 miles again the next week, and then try 15-18 miles, and then 20 miles. If you are a more experienced runner who runs 30-40 miles a week, and you are used to running 10 miles at a time, start your marathon training long runs with 13 miles, then try 16-17 miles the next week, then drop back to 13 miles the next week, then do 17 miles again the next week, then 20 miles the week after that. The week after a 20-mile run, make your "long run" 10-13 miles, or less if you are new to long distances and you still feel tired. Repeat this pattern at least one more time before the marathon, working up to a second 20-mile run and then backing down. Of course you don't have to do your long runs on the weekends, but that is usually the time when people have a few hours to spend. But if you have Wednesday mornings free, and that's a better time for you than Saturday morning, adjust your training schedule accordingly.

48| Avoid New Shoe Blues, Break Them In Early

Don't wear new shoes to run a marathon. To give your feet the best advantage, put at least 100 miles on your running shoes prior to the marathon. Even if your shoes feel great the first day you put them on (which they should) and even if you're putting on a pair of shoes that's identical to your previous pair, a break-in period lets you be sure that you have the right size, and you can get used to the feel of the new shoes and reduce your risk of blisters. And, if for some reason you realize that the current pair rubs in a strange way, and just isn't going to work, you have time to buy and break in another pair before marathon day.

49| Don't Buy Into Brand Hype

Resist the temptation to buy a certain brand or style just because you like the color, or because your favorite sports star is wearing it. Wearing the wrong shoe style or size for your foot is one of the top causes of running injuries. If you're new to running, new to marathoning, or experiencing foot pain, seek out a local specialty running store, rather than a chain store, and try some different shoes, and promise yourself to buy what fits your feet. no matter what color it is. The staff members at specialty running stores usually know their stuff and can help you choose a shoe. Road Runner Sports (and some specialty running stores) will take shoes back and let you exchange them if you aren't happy with them once you have worn them for a few days, or a few weeks. Remember, you won't be looking at your feet while you are running, anyway, so if the right shoe for you is a color that clashes with your shorts, you won't see it most of the time. And the best news is, most shoe companies change the colors several times a year, so you'll only have those blaze orange Nikes for a few months.

50| Mars And Venus In The Shoe Store

Running shoes, like any other shoes, are available in men's and women's styles and sizes. The men's and women's styles of the same model usually have the same attributes, such as extra cushioning or stability. Some models of women's shoes are cut slightly narrower, and women with wide or large feet may want to try on a men's model of a shoe they like; they may find a better fit.

51| Tap Your Heels For Perfect Shoe Fit

After you slide your foot into your running shoe, point your foot at about a 45-degree angle to the floor and tap your heel 2-3 times. This action helps ensure that your heel is flush against the inside of the shoe before you tighten the laces, and it will help keep your heels from slipping.

Also, I recommend double-knotting your shoelaces, not only for a more secure fit but to avoid the annoyance of stopping to tie your shoes in the middle of a run.

52| Orthotics: They May Be The Support You Need

A pair of orthotics can alleviate many of the foot and leg problems marathoners experience. If you have chronic pain in your foot, ankle, knee, hip, or back, it's worth a visit to the podiatrist. You may pronate (your ankle tips to the inside) or supinate (your ankle tips to the outside). Check the injuries chapter for more details on these conditions, but simply put, if your foot rolls around when it strikes the ground, especially over the long miles of marathon training, you are at increased risk for injuries, and orthotics may help. Check the American Academy of Podiatric Sports Medicine website at aapsm.org for ideas if you don't have a regular podiatrist, or ask fellow runners in your area for a recommendation. If you don't like what you hear from a podiatrist, such as "just don't run," then run, don't walk, to another podiatrist. The right doctor wants to help keep you healthy and happily running and there are ways to correct almost all foot problems. Most custom made orthotics (ordered through a podiatrist) cost several hundred dollars, but some insurance companies will cover one pair per calendar year, and once you have them they will last for several years. That said, some runners do just fine with simple over-the-counter arch supports or shoe insoles from a drug store, and a podiatrist can customize these devices with extra padding in a way that gives your feet the support they need.

53| Recycling Running Shoes: When The Bag In The Closet Overflows

Let's face it, how many old running shoes do you need to keep around to mow the lawn? Probably just one. Maybe two. So, what to do with all those running shoes that you have dutifully "retired" from running after 350-500 miles of running? If all else fails, you can probably donate them to your local United Way or Salvation Army. Or, ask at the specialty running store in your area. Some stores, and some running clubs, collect used shoes periodically and send them to charities overseas. The bottom line is: Don't run in old shoes because you think they will be wasted. You can find a way to give them new life without risking injury.

54| Rotate Your Shoes

It may seem excessive, but once you find a shoe you like, buy a second pair right away. Rotating between two pairs of shoes not only ensures that you have backup of a shoe you like, but it's better for your feet and legs not to wear the same shoes for running day in and day out for several months. When you first put on a new pair of shoes, write the date on the bottom, so you know when you started wearing them. After about a month or so of regular wear, start breaking in a second pair ("pair B") on shorter weekday runs (and write the date on that pair, too) and wear the older pair for long runs. Once "pair A" has close to 200 miles on it, or if you feel that the cushioning or stability is deteriorating, switch and use pair A for weekday short runs again, and move pair B to the long weekend training runs. Retire your shoes when they have 350-500 miles on them. Once you have retired pair A, it's time to purchase another pair, and repeat the rotation pattern. Even if they don't look worn out, the midsole support and cushioning will have broken down by then, and the shoes won't be protecting your feet.

55| The Care And Feeding Of Running Shoes

You ask a lot of your running shoes when you are training for a marathon, so get the most out of them by treating them right. When you finish a run, remove your orthotics (if you have them) and keep them somewhere other than inside the shoes. This allows both orthotics and shoes to dry out, which will help them last longer than if they are perpetually damp. When your shoes are wet, either from excessive sweat or a rainy run, stuff a page or two of newspaper in each shoe and leave it there. When you go to put your shoes on the next day, pull out the paper and you'll find that the paper is damp but your shoes will be dry. Don't put running shoes in the washer and dryer. If your shoes are dirty and muddy enough to bother you, use an old toothbrush or rag and scrub them off in a sink, and allow them to air dry (or use the newspaper technique). The hot air dryer will speed up the breakdown of the shoes' material, and you'll be wearing them out soon enough.

56| Think Big, Size Up When Buying Running Shoes

In general, the right size running shoe is a half to a full size larger than your everyday shoes, depending on the style of the shoe and whether you have any insoles or orthotics to insert. For example, my everyday shoe size varies from 8.5 to 9, but my current running shoe is a 10, in part because I have to accommodate my orthotics. If you're torn between two sizes, choose the larger. Your feet will expand when running long distances (and even short distances). You can always add an insole or wear thicker socks to fine-tune the fit, but you want to be sure to have about a thumb width of space between the end of your big toe and the end of the shoe.

57| Use A Lace-Locking Technique For A Better Shoe Fit

If you have narrow heels that tend to slip in your running shoes, a simple shoe-lacing strategy will help keep your feet snugly in place and prevent blisters.

- Lace your shoes normally until you get to the hole one down from the top.
- Bring the lace through this hole so it is on the outside of the shoe.
- Then, instead of crossing the lace over, put it through the topmost hole, going from the outside of the shoe to the inside. This creates a small loop.
- Don't pull it tight, leave a small loop.
- Repeat on the opposite side of the shoe.
- When you have two loops, take the end of the lace on the left side of the shoe (which should be pointing towards the inside of the shoe) and thread it through the loop on the right; then take the end of the lace on the right side of the shoe (which also should be pointing towards the inside of the shoe) and thread it through the loop on the left side.
- Put the shoe on, and pull on the ends of the laces, which will pull the loops flat against the shoe.
- Tie your usual bow and you're ready to go.

58| Your Arch Type Points You To The Right Style Of Shoe

Most manufacturers base their running shoe designs on three categories based on the arch of the foot: low arch, average arch, and high arch.

- Low arch: If you have fleet feet and low arches, you need a more stable shoe to guide your foot's motion, so look for "stability shoes."
- High arch: If you have a high arch, you want a neutral shoe to keep your feet aligned and plenty of cushioning to absorb the shock of your footfalls. Look for "cushioned" shoes.
- Average arch: If you have an average arch, you need a shoe with some stability, but not too much, you can wear almost any shoe, and your best bet will depend on whether your average arch falls on the high or low side of average. If you're on the high side of average, try cushioned shoes first. A stability shoe might not flex enough, and it could cause you to develop plantar fasciitis (more about that in the injury section).

If you're not sure what type of arch you have, put a piece of paper on the bathroom floor and check out the shape of your wet foot when you get out of the shower. If you see a very narrow mark between your toes and heels, you have a high arch. If you see a large, flat patch, you have low arches.

59| Cold Weather Gear: The 20-Degree Rule

Some people prefer to run inside on a treadmill when the temperature drops. But if that's not an option or if you just like to run outside, here's a good rule of thumb: Dress for 20 degrees warmer than the thermometer says. If it's in the 25 degrees Fahrenheit, for example, it will feel like 45 degrees (more or less, depending on the wind). If you feel a bit chilly for the first 1-2 miles, you'll probably be comfortable during most of your run. The key to staying comfortable is lightweight layers, rather than one heavy layer. Start with a moisture-wicking shirt and add another shirt on top of that. If it is really cold add a running jacket that is breathable, but also has some wind and water resistance. If you live in the north, choose a jacket with less breathability and more wind resistance to keep you warmer. In a moderate climate, choose a jacket with more breathability. I recommend owning one item of several types of outerwear: A lightweight vest, a breathable but water-resistant jacket, and a windbreaker that's less breathable but keeps out more wind and water.

60| Cotton Is Rotten For Running Clothes: Choose Moisture-Wicking Fabrics

Fortunately for marathoners, sports apparel has come a long way from the cotton t-shirt. You can wear almost anything to run a few miles, but a marathon is different. You'll be running for hours, and moisture-wicking clothing can make a difference in your comfort and in your ability to race and focus on other things, like keeping your pace and enjoying the experience. Different apparel manufacturers have different names for their moisture-wicking fabric, including Dri-Fit from Nike, ClimaCool from Adidas, and almost any gear from Under Armour. If you want to spend a little less, Road Runner Sports, online at roadrunnersports.com, has its own line of apparel made from moisture-wicking fabric that is reasonably priced and high-quality; look for DryRoad or DryLine on the label.

61| Don't Knock Your Socks

You can get away with almost any sport sock if you're running a few miles, but if you're training for a marathon, your feet will thank you if you don't skimp on socks. Good quality padded, moisture-wicking socks will last for a few years (believe it or not), depending on how much you wear them, and it is worth the money to get a few pairs. Some running socks have additional padding in the heel and forefoot, which makes them more comfortable for those 20-mile training runs. If you have orthotics and you need to remove the cushioned insole that comes in your shoes, padded socks can replace some of that lost cushioning. The moisture-wicking trait is especially important because sweaty or wet feet are more likely to blister. When you are trying on a new make or model of shoes, bring the socks that you usually train in with you, and see how they fit. For the marathon, thick socks are a good bet. Unless you are running at a 6-minute pace and wearing lightweight racing shoes, thicker socks will provide some additional cushioning over the long miles of the marathon.

62| Here Comes The Sun

If you're out on a long training run for 2-3 hours during the spring, summer, or fall, use a sweatproof sunblock to help prevent a painful sunburn the next day. Although you'll probably sweat some of it off on a hot, humid day, a sweatproof formula sunblock stands up to sweat much better than a standard formula. Many skin care manufacturers including offer sweat-resistant sunblocks at prices ranging from less than $10 a bottle to $30 or more. You don't have to spend a lot on sunblock, but make sure you use a lot. Don't forget the backs of your legs and the back of your neck.

63| Running Apparel Care: Cold Wash, Air Dry

Washing running apparel in cold water on the delicate cycle (with a gentle detergent such as Woolite) will prolong its life. And hang running clothes to dry. Because they are made of moisture-wicking fabric, they will dry within a few hours and they'll be ready for your next run. Wash your running socks in your choice of warm or cold water and dry them in the dryer, even moisture-wicking socks. Putting running socks in the dryer makes them softer and more comfortable, and in my experience machine-drying doesn't seem to wear out the fabric in socks the way it can in other sports apparel.

64| Pick Apparel With Pockets

Shorts or shirts with zip or mesh pockets are perfect for carrying gels on a long run or during a marathon. Some runners like belts or backpacks with slots for water bottles, energy bars and gels, and other odds and ends like tissues or Advil. But I recommend pockets because a belt is one more thing that will be rubbing against you for 26 miles, and there's the possibility of chafing and blistering, even if you wear it regularly, because the belt doesn't conform to the shape of your body over time. Plus, marathons will have water stops, so unless you are carrying your favorite energy drink, there's no need to tote your own water. But beware of key pockets. I won't trust my keys to a pocket unless there is a zipper or Velcro. If you have to carry keys on a long run or marathon, take only the key or keys you need and use a safety pin to pin them inside the waistband of your shorts, or pin it inside the mesh pocket.

65| Running Shirts: Choose Any Style In A Fabric With Substance

Depending on the weather and on your level of modesty, you will be running in a long-sleeved shirt, short-sleeved shirt, tank top, or just a sports bra. If you like V-neck t-shirts, choose one. If you like mock turtlenecks, that's fine. There's no right or wrong when it comes to style, but it is the substance of the shirt that counts. Moisture-wicking fabrics are essential, especially in a shirt, since a shirt will be in direct contact with your skin. If you haven't worn moisture-wicking shirts to work out, you are in for a treat, and if you have, use your marathon training as an excuse to buy another one. You should have at least two long-sleeved moisture-wicking shirts and two-short sleeved shirts on hand, so no matter what the season, you have a dry shirt and a spare. These shirts aren't cheap, but you can find good deals if you shop around or buy long- or short-sleeves at the end of the season, when stores are bringing in new merchandise and catalogs such as championcatalog.com and roadrunnersports.com have clearance items. If you take care of your running shirts, they will last for years because they don't wear out as quickly as shorts or tights, which are subject to more friction.

66| The Long And Short Of Running Shorts

You can wear almost any style of shorts for most runs of 5 miles or less, but if you are running longer distances and training for a marathon, chafing becomes an important factor. Choose the wrong shorts and you may be uncomfortable at best, and distracted by painful chafing at worst. Your running shorts should add to your comfort, not add to your discomfort. I find most shorts bunch up on me when I run, so I wear fitted, cycling-style shorts. Depending on how much leg you want to show, you can find fitted shorts (or baggy shorts) with inseams ranging from 2 or 3 inches to 9 inches. Many men's shorts styles have breathable liners for extra comfort.

67| Tights, Or Not So Tight

When it's cold, running tights are a runner's best friend, especially if you are out for two hours on a long training run. But if you don't feel comfortable in body-hugging tights, don't despair. Most manufacturers offer several styles of running pants, including boot-cut and wide-leg styles. But the same principle holds true for running pants as for shorts; excess fabric can bunch up and cause chafing. Try on running pants on with your running shoes to be sure that your boot legs or wide legs aren't dragging on the ground, where you might trip on them.

68| Watching Your Clock

A basic stopwatch is a useful tool and helpful for all marathon runners. If you are not sure of a distance, or if you are traveling, you can use your watch and just run for half and hour, or an hour, depending on your training schedule. And you can get a general sense of how you're feeling by comparing how long it takes you to run the same route under different whether conditions, and when you've had different amounts of rest the night or nights before. You don't need a $100 watch to do that. You can buy a simple stop watch almost anywhere, from a department store to a catalog or a sporting goods store, and even an expensive model should last for several years.

69| Women: If The Bra Fits, Wear It

Training for a marathon involves running for hours at a time, and if you have an ill-fitting sports bra, you will know it by the chafe marks you'll see (and feel) after the run. If you don't already have a favorite sports bra, try on a few styles and find one that feels comfortable in the store. If it's not comfortable when you put it on, it probably won't feel comfortable after 15 miles of running. But it should feel snug; you don't want to be bouncing. Read the labels and make sure that the bra advertises maximum support for the cup sizes. If your local store doesn't have a spectrum of sizes and styles that appeal to you, user-friendly online resources include championcatalog.com and roadrunnersports.com. Ideally, don't wear a brand new bra on the day of a race or a long run. Test it out on short runs first, and if you're not happy with it, either exchange it, or if it is comfortable but not supportive enough for running, keep it to use for the gym or yoga or another low-impact activity.

70| Carbo-Loading: Not Just For Marathon Day

The principle of loading up on carbohydrates the night before a marathon is a good one in theory, but it's important not to get carried away. I recommend having a high-carbohydrate meal, such as pasta or pizza (I usually have pizza) the night before your weekly long training runs. A high-carb dinner will stay with you through the run the next morning. If you do your long runs in the afternoon or evening, have a high-carb snack, such as a bagel or leftover pizza (if there is any) a few hours before you run. Experiment with different foods now and then, or see how you feel if you go out to dinner the night before a long training run and have something unusual. If you know what makes you feel energized but not bloated or sluggish because you've eaten it before your long runs, you can eat that same thing, or something similar, the night before the marathon. During the week prior to the marathon, eat as you normally do. It's not really necessary to load up on pasta 3 days before the marathon, because it will be out of your system. Also, since you will be running much less than usual during the last week before the race, eating as usual will create some carbo-loading by default because you aren't burning as many carbohydrates by running.

71| Don't Fall for Fad Diets: Use Common Sense

Running in general--and training for a marathon in particular--takes energy, and that comes from food. The important thing is not to obsess about food, and try to eat a balanced diet, and the most important thing is to eat. Eat plenty of carbohydrates; they remain a marathoner's first-line energy source. Some fat is important, too, so it's OK to put real butter or cream cheese on your bagel if that's what you like, and be sure to incorporate healthy fats (aka monounsaturated or polyunsaturated fats), into your food plan. Some easy sources of these healthy fats are olive oil, flaxseed, walnuts and most other nuts, and cold-water fish such as salmon and herring.

72| Don't Forget Your Beta Carotene

Although it has not been widely studied, evidence suggests that beta carotene may enhance athletic performance. Runner's World has published several stories about recommended foods for runners, and most of those stories include a few beta carotene-rich foods. They can't hurt and beta carotene is good for you from a nutritional standpoint, even if it doesn't shave minutes off your marathon time. Pumpkin is a great source of beta carotene, and you can find many pumpkin-filled foods to enjoy in the fall when you're training for a fall marathon. Carrots and papaya are other good sources (think orange), so carrot cake and carrot muffins count, too. Quick breads and muffins, especially if they are made in part with whole-wheat flour, are a great snack for runners while marathon training or at any time, but add the carrot or pumpkin and the nutritional payoff is even bigger. If you like to cook, quick breads and muffins are easy to make and most cookbooks and websites have a variety of recipes, depending on your personal taste. Not a cook? Look for pumpkin items at your favorite bakery.

73| Don't Run On Empty

To prepare for daily runs, even for distances of 5 miles or so, you'll probably feel better if you eat something before you go out. What you have, and how much, depends in part on the time of day when you run. I'm a morning runner, and so most of the time I have a banana, and I confess that I do sometimes eat something sugary if it's available. I have a sweet tooth, and I know a piece or two of Halloween candy won't bother me on a short run. Before my long training runs, I like to squirt some honey on the banana for extra quick energy. Bananas have long been a favorite of endurance athletes because they digest easily and provide potassium for your hard-working muscles. And the honey provides sugar and carbs for quick energy and nice flavor. Try some different snacks during your training runs to see what makes you feel the most energetic. If caffeine disagrees with you, avoid it, or introduce caffeinated gels or drinks gradually.

74| Eating On The Run: Helpful For Marathons And Marathon Training

Some studies have shown that honey is just as effective as gel in providing energy during endurance events, but since it's not well packaged for carrying on the run, the preference is energy gel. During long training runs, which I define as more than 13 miles, I usually carry 1-2 gel packets with me, but I know some runners who go through 3-4 gel packs on a 16-20 mile run. Take more with you than you think you'll need. You can save the unopened packs for the next run. When I ran my first marathon, energy bars and gels were in their infancy, and all I consumed during my first marathon was water every 5 miles or so. But research has shown, and my experience agrees, that eating something during the marathon can help stave off muscle cramps and give you a boost of energy. Of course, if you haven't trained well, don't expect 10 packs of gel to save you from fatigue, but strategically slurping one or two, especially in the first half of the marathon, before you think you need them, has helped me in many marathons.

75| Energy Drinks vs. Water: Your Choice

Many marathoners prefer to replace lost nutrients during long runs and marathons by consuming energy drinks such as Gatorade, Excel, or other products. These drinks provide the same benefits as energy bars or gels. But a gel is more concentrated, and you may have to drink more of an energy drink to get the same amount of nutrients as you would get from a slurp of gel. But as with other marathon day activities, don't drink something during the marathon that you haven't tried during training. Many marathons offer lesser-known brands of sports drinks, rather than a big name like Gatorade. The formulas for these drinks are similar, but not identical, and just because you like Gatorade on your training runs, doesn't mean that the unfamiliar sports drink available at the marathon water stop will agree with you You can have both gel and sports drinks; there's no rule against that. But be sure to consume some liquid along with the energy gel to promote the absorption of the nutrients into your body. I do recommend drinking some type of sports drink after a very long run (16-20 miles) to help replenish lost nutrients immediately. In my experience, a post-run sports drink tastes good and makes me feel better after a long run, and that's enough of a reason to try it.

76| Energy Gels And Bars: Experiment To Find Your Favorite

Once upon a time, there were no energy bars and gels. My father ran a marathon in 1980 and recalls carrying lime slices tucked into his headband. Today, you can choose from an array of brands and flavors of energy bars and gels. The gels may not be as tasty as the bars, but they are easier to slurp down and chase with water at a water stop during a marathon, rather than trying to chew something. Besides, an energy bar can freeze solid on winter training runs and you don't need to spend your time (and energy) gnawing at a frozen bar. That said, many of the energy bars make great snacks, especially if you're looking for something in the afternoon to see you through a late-day workout. Which bar or gel is the best for marathons? The best one is the one that agrees with your stomach, and comes in a flavor that you like. Honestly, we aren't eating these things because they are delicious, we're eating them for the nutrition replacement. But the flavors of energy bars and gels continue to improve, so try different flavors and brands on long runs to see what suits your stomach. My personal favorite is Power Gel, in either the chocolate or tangerine flavors (both have caffeine). Read the labels on bars and gels. Some contain caffeine, some even contain "double caffeine" and some have no caffeine. Although caffeine has been shown to have some benefits for endurance athletes, some people are sensitive to it, and if you don't regularly consume caffeine, you may want to try a caffeine-free gel or bar first.

77| Good, Good, Good, Good Hydration

You may have heard about runners dying from hyponatremia (excessive hydration), but that doesn't mean you should go to the other extreme and not drink enough water. Even in cold weather, if you are running much more than 10-12 miles, be sure to have at least a few sips of water a few times during the run. Cold air, especially wind, is dehydrating, and you will get thirsty during a 16-20 mile run, even if it's only 20 degrees outside. Remember that most energy gels and bars need to be eaten with some water to help the nutrients get into the bloodstream and do you some good. The amount of water you drink is individual, and as you do longer runs, try drinking 1/2 cup of water every 4-8 miles. If it's hot, you will need more, if it's cold, you'll need less, but everyone's hydration needs are different and it's important to experiment during training so you know what works for marathon day. There are formulas to calculate how much you should drink based on weighing yourself before and after workouts, but I find that listening to your body, plus some trial and error, works just as well, especially because the weather will have a significant impact on your hydration needs.

78| Indulgences: Don't Demonize Food

I am a devout runner, but I also have a huge sweet tooth, and I have great respect for the late chef and food-lover Julia Child, who advocated moderate amounts of "real food" such as real butter, and exhorted people to enjoy their food. "Fat gives things flavor," she reportedly said. Of course, people with specific health and food issues need to be mindful of those issues, and if you are on a weight-loss diet different rules apply, but this is a marathon training book, not a diet book. In fact, with all the energy you're expending, it's OK to indulge in pretty much anything you like, with a dash of common sense. You don't need to make a habit out of eating a whole pint of ice cream daily, but in my experience most runners, especially marathoners, can splurge on weekends and it won't show up on the scale. Some of your favorite things may have little or no nutritional value, so keep those things to a minimum and don't neglect the genuinely healthy food. I tend to indulge in dessert and peanut butter. By contrast, one of my training partners, who shall remain anonymous, likes to indulge in a trip to KFC periodically for a bucket of chicken and biscuits. Disclaimer: I am not a professional nutritionist, but it's ok to enjoy a drink or dessert. If you over-indulge, forgive yourself and go for a nice run the next day.

79| Protein Power

Protein is essential for distance running (and for good health in general), but use common sense and don't abandon carbohydrates and fats in favor of a high-protein diet. Nutritionist Liz Applegate, Ph.D., a regular contributor to Runner's World magazine, has a sensible approach to nutrition. She suggests that runners consume about 15 percent of their daily calories as protein, which is about half the amount of protein suggested by high-protein diets. Most marathoners will burn carbohydrates and fats first during long runs, but after an hour or so of running your body will be looking for another energy source and will start burning protein, so you do need it in your diet. If you're a vegetarian, know your alternative protein sources. Protein is essential to muscle recovery as well, so it's not only tasty, but healthy, to indulge that post-workout craving for peanut butter, or a hamburger, or your favorite protein to help your muscles refuel and prepare for the next workout.

80| Vegetarian Marathoners: Know Your Proteins

If you're a vegetarian training for a marathon, be sure to read up on your alternative proteins, because protein is important for muscle maintenance and recovery (see *Protein Power* tip). Vitamins and supplements won't hurt, but don't depend on them. Most nutritionists agree that it's best not to rely on vitamins or nutritional supplements at the expense of real food, because there are components of foods that interact with each other in ways we don't fully understand. From a marathon training perspective, the most important thing is to eat enough, and try to eat a variety of foods. As you increase your mileage, you may find yourself craving more protein, whether it is peanut butter or something else, so have some! Your muscles will thank you. Runner's World is a great nutrition information resource for runners, and includes vegetarian recipes and snacks that appeal to non-vegetarians, too.

81| Bring Extra Warmup/Cooldown Clothes For Weather Changes

Wear warm-up clothes before the start of the marathon, and pack them in a bag that you can check or leave in your car so you can put on something warm and dry after the race. Depending on the marathon, you may or may not be in a place where you can change your clothes, but swapping a sweaty shirt for a dry one on a hot day or putting a fleece top over your race shirt on a cold day will make you more comfortable on the way home. Even though you have chosen your likely clothing for the marathon, bring other options in case of a sudden weather change. If you think that you will wear a long-sleeved shirt, bring a short-sleeved shirt, too, and vice versa. You can pack anything you don't wear in a bag to check at the start or leave in your car. If you have space in your bag, bring an extra pair of shoes and socks. Your feet will thank you if you can slip them into something different after several hours of running in the same pair of shoes. Although the moisture-wicking socks should keep your feet dry, it feels great to put on a different pair of socks to travel home. Also, if you have developed a blister or a black toenail or some other foot problem, putting on different shoes and socks to travel home will provide some relief until you can take care of the problem.

82| Bring Throwaway Layers

A marathon is a long race, and it is often as much as 20 degrees colder at the start than it will be at the finish several hours later. To keep comfortable on a chilly morning, bring a throwaway t-shirt to wear as an extra layer for the first mile or two, or for however long it takes you to feel comfortable. You can use one of those old cotton t-shirts that you don't wear for running; you will discard it before it gets clammy. If you can't part with any t-shirts from previous races, an old undershirt or an old windbreaker will do, as will a trash bag (see tip on trash bags for details).

83| Eat In Advance

Most marathons start in the morning, and you don't have time to digest a big breakfast, but eating something before the race helps jump-start your muscles and calm a nervous stomach. Your best bet is to eat what you usually eat before your long runs. Try a banana with some honey and a cup of tea (also with a bit of honey). If the race is later than 10 a.m. and you ate early and feel hungry, snack on an energy bar an hour or so before the start. Drink some water, but resist the urge to over-hydrate. Even on a hot day, your body can only process so much, and you don't want to make excessive pit stops during the marathon.

84| No Sleep? No Worries

Many marathoners, even the experienced ones, don't sleep well the night before the marathon. You may be nervous, excited, or both. But don't worry. Get a good night's sleep for a night or two before that last night, and you'll be just as well off than if you slept soundly the night before (not that there's anything wrong with that). On marathon day you'll have adrenaline to make up for lost sleep. And you will probably sleep soundly for the next few nights after the marathon.

85| Post-Race Protocol

After the marathon, congratulate yourself! You made it to the finish line and that is an accomplishment, regardless of your finishing time. Your first acts should include drinking some water or other liquid, turning in your timing chip (if chips are being used) and retrieving your bag. And wrap up in the lightweight "space blankets" that most marathon volunteers will give you at the finish along with your finisher's medal. You'll be surprised how quickly you can develop a chill, even on a warm day. If the marathon is using timing chips, race volunteers are almost always available at the finish to help you remove the chip from your shoe. Make sure to turn in your chip or your time won't be recorded! If you are ill or injured, look for the medical tent. If you are not ill or injured, get the free post-race massage if it is available, and if you can make the time. Even smaller marathons often have volunteers from local massage schools or physical therapy practices who have set up a tent to tend to marathoners. Ideally, retrieve your bag first, so you can put on something dry while standing in line. You will usually get about 7-10 minutes of easy massage on your legs, back, and shoulders (you stay dressed for this). Even a few minutes of massage helps promote circulation and restores your tired muscles, and you will feel less stiff the next day. If you're traveling home from the marathon by plane, the massage is an especially good idea because nothing promotes stiff legs like sitting in an airplane seat.

86| Trash Bag: Don't Leave Home Without It

Believe it or not, a trash bag is the world's greatest disposable windbreaker. I keep one with my pre-marathon bag and bring it with me even when I know I won't need to wear it. I wore one for the entire Harrisburg Marathon in 2006 during windy and rainy conditions, and I was surprisingly comfortable wearing a moisture-wicking short-sleeved shirt and shorts underneath the bag, along with a pair of lightweight cotton-blend gloves. Here's how to wear your bag in style: Punch a hole in the bottom of the bag and rip an opening large enough to put your head through. Then poke a hole in each side at about shoulder height for your arms, and you're set to go. Once you start to feel warm, after 1 mile, 5 miles, or at any point, simply grab the bag up near your neck and rip it down the front when you approach the next water stop, and toss it off to the side. As a courtesy to your fellow runners, make sure you toss the bag onto the side of the road so no one near you slips on it.

87| Travel Smart: Allow Extra Time

When traveling to a marathon, whether you have a short drive or a long trip to the airport to catch a flight, leave more time than you think you'll need. You will have enough on your mind without the stress of being late. Before you close your suitcase, review your race clothes, with a few choices of shirts and shorts for different weather conditions, and your warm-up/cool-down clothes. Double-check to make sure that you have your favorite accessories, such as a sweatband, hat, watch, and packets of gel. If your race is local, set out your likely race clothes, alternative clothes, and warm-up/cool-down clothes so you don't have to think about what to put on when you wake up on race day.

88| Warm Up, But Don't Wear Out

You don't need an excessive warm-up before running a marathon the way you might before a 5K or 10K race. Stick to your usual pre-run stretching routine, and if jogging around for 5 minutes or so helps calm your nerves, that's OK. But resist the urge to spend too much time warming up; you don't want to wear yourself out. If you are anxious, use the time to do more stretching instead. And especially in a large marathon, the start will be so crowded that you will be running slower than your ideal pace for the first mile or two, which serves as a warm-up. This can be blessing in disguise because it keeps you from running too fast at the start.

89| What If Something Goes Wrong?

A marathon is a long way to run, and anything can happen. Bad things do happen, even to good runners. If you become ill or injured during a marathon, seek help at the next water stop. If the problem is minor, such as a side stitch or stomach cramp, walk for a few minutes, breathing deeply. If you have a muscle spasm or a muscle feels tight, pull over to the side of the road and stretch. Don't panic. Walk as much as you need to. There is no reason to worsen a potentially serious injury just to meet your goal time or to finish. If you can finish by alternating running and walking, that's fine. But if the injury or illness is extreme, you may have to seek care at a water stop or first aid station. You'll be frustrated, but remember that you can always train for another marathon and use what you have learned during the training process to avoid problems in your next race.

90| Your Marathon Day Kit

The night before the marathon, pack a small bag that you can check at the start and retrieve at the finish. Some marathons provide bags that you are required to use if you want to check them at the start. In that case, be sure to use that bag or you will not be allowed to check your gear. Make sure the bag has a tag with your race number on it. Many marathons provide a matching baggage tag that accompanies every runner's race number. You can detach this smaller tag and put it on the bag that you'll check at the start. What should you put in this bag? Eventually your warm-up/cool-down clothes will go in it. But also pack your alternative race clothing options, and a Ziploc bag with the following:

- Band-aids in a few different sizes
- Pain reliever of choice (Advil, Tylenol)
- Sweatproof sunblock
- Tissues
- Moist towelettes/wet wipes
- Extra pins for your race number
- A small towel, especially if it is rainy, to mop off after the race

Don't forget your race number. Some marathons require you to pick up your race number (and timing chip, if chips are used). Make sure to pin your race number to your shirt and thread the chip through your shoelace.

91| Basic First Aid Revisited

Most people know the maxim RICE: Rest, Ice, Compression, and Elevation. This basic first-aid principle applies to most running injuries. From a runner's perspective, rest can mean no running, or it can mean a shorter run. Ice means putting ice on the sore spot, using an Ace bandage for compression and for holding the ice pack in place. Elevation may not be possible depending on the injury, but if you have a foot injury and you can spend 20 minutes lying down with your foot elevated above the level of your heart, you will promote circulation and help with healing. I would add an M to this acronym, for mobility. Once the swelling decreases, start some stretching exercises to increase the circulation to the injured area and cut down on the formation of scar tissue.

92| Battling Blisters

Blisters may be the most common of all running injuries, but they are among the easiest problems to treat and prevent with no long-term ill effects. If you have a small blister that is not too painful, cover it with a bandage and go on with your day. The blister will probably rupture on its own. But if you have a larger blister that is painful, you may need to drain it. If it is very large (more than an inch) and severe, you may want to see your podiatrist, but you can take care of small blisters yourself with these steps:

- Get some cotton balls, a safety pin, rubbing alcohol, and a band-aid.
- Clean the blistered area with rubbing alcohol using individual alcohol wipes or an alcohol-soaked cotton ball.
- Use another wipe or cotton ball to clean the pointy tip of the safety pin.
- Gently poke the pin into the edge of the blister where you feel the most liquid underneath and push on the area gently to coax as much fluid out of the pinhole as possible. Blot the area with a tissue or cotton ball and put a band-aid over it.

I recommend leaving the band-aid on during your next run, and replacing it after you shower. This method works for small, uncomplicated blisters, but if the area is discolored, extremely painful, or large, see your podiatrist. Blisters are caused by friction and that friction can come from an ill-fitting shoe, a bunched up sock, or damp, sweaty feet in shoes that don't wick the moisture well enough on a hot day. If you have a chronic problem with blisters, check the fit of your shoe or sock. Your foot may be sliding too much in your shoe (see the lacing tip in the shoe section).

93| Ease Achy Muscles

Not all running injuries are serious. Here are few tips to manage the minor aches and pains that are part of training for a marathon:

- When you feel especially stiff after a tough workout, fill a bathtub with warm water and add 3-4 cups of Epsom salt, which you can buy at most grocery stores or drugstores. Soak for 15 minutes, and you will notice a difference the next day.
- Muscle rubs such as Biofreeze and the arnica gels sold at health food stores can provide topical, short-term relief of minor aches. But if you have severe, persistent muscle pain, seek professional advice.
- Ice. You can rarely go wrong putting ice on a sore spot.
- Heat. Don't use a heating pad on an area that is red or swollen, but placing a heating pad behind your back or sitting on a heating pad at work can relieve low back or upper hamstring stiffness. But limit heating pad use to 15 minutes a few times daily to avoid skin irritation.

94| Ice With Veggies

Almost any running injury, major or minor, will feel better if you put ice on the area. You can buy commercial ice packs, but a bag of frozen peas is the most effective ice pack available because it conforms easily to the shape of your foot, leg, elbow, or any other injured area. You can reuse the same bag until it falls apart. Just make sure to label the peas with a marker of some sort so no one cooks and eats them by mistake! The most effective way to ice an injury is to apply ice to the injured area at 10-15 minute intervals. After 15-20 minutes, the ice pack starts to warm up and lose its effectiveness, so return it to the freezer and ice the spot again in a few hours. Put ice on an injury as soon as possible after activity, or any time that is convenient.

95| Leg-Length Difference Can Cause Back And Hip Pain

Most people are not perfectly symmetrical, we have one leg that is slightly shorter than the other. But marathon training will introduce you to your biomechanical flaws. When I was training for my first marathon and running distances longer than 12 miles for the first time, I developed severe pain in my upper left hip, just below the waist. I could barely walk. I called my podiatrist, who recommended a chiropractor or an orthopedist. I went with the chiropractor, but what you need is someone who can take an x-ray and determine whether you have a leg-length discrepancy. If you have a difference of a quarter inch (4-5 mm) or more, a heel lift in the shorter foot will solve the problem, although you may need to wear the lift of the same height in your everyday shoes as well as your running shoes to avoid re-injury.

96| Neuromas: Surgery Is The Best Treatment

Surgery is a last resort for most running injuries. But if you reach a point where conservative methods fail and you want to continue running, surgery may be necessary. In some cases, a simple surgery is the easiest and most effective treatment. A neuroma is a common foot injury for which surgery provides the most effective long-term solution. A neuroma occurs when the bones of the foot move in a way that causes a nerve to shear off and start forming a piece of scar tissue. Over time, the piece of scar tissue will become larger, and eventually it becomes large enough to press on the nerve and cause pain. You may have a neuroma if you notice a tingling sensation every time you step, but there are no outward signs of redness or swelling. The most common site for a neuroma is between the third and fourth toes, although it can occur anywhere in the foot. Non-runners develop neuromas, too. Some people can get sufficient relief by wearing wider shoes or by getting an occasional cortisone shot, but the most effective treatment, especially for runners, is a short, outpatient procedure in which the foot surgeon uses a pair of surgical scissors to cut out the neuroma. If you have surgery for any kind of running injury, get a recommendation for a surgeon who has experience in dealing with athletes, and pay attention to the surgeon's instructions about post-operative care. You can cross train by walking, biking, or pool running after many types of surgery, but be sure to return to running gradually. If you have dissolvable stitches (which are used in neuroma surgery), avoid excessive stress (such as running) on the area until the stitches have dissolved, which takes about 6 weeks.

97| Non-Running Injuries: When To Run Through Them

You can run with a strain, but don't try to run on a sprain. A sprained ankle will be swollen and warm to the touch, and it will hurt much more than a strain. If you have a strain, you can run, but modify your training until it feels better. That may mean skipping speed work and sticking to short, easy runs, or trading the planned 17-mile weekend long run for a 13-mile run, but your training won't suffer. As always, listen to your body, and if the pain persists, visit a sports medicine professional to address the problem and take a day or two off from running. Similarly, you can run with a mild head cold, and I have found that an easy run helps to relieve congestion. But if you are seriously ill, stay home. A good rule of thumb: If you are sick from the neck up, you can probably run, but if you are sick from the next down (a respiratory or gastrointestinal illness) stay home and recover, and see your doctor if necessary.

98| Painkillers: The Power Of Three

If you have an acute injury or a flare-up of a chronic problem, and ibuprofen doesn't bother you, take 3 Advil 3 times daily for 3 days. I'm not a doctor, but my podiatrist recommended this regimen to me for an acute tendon inflammation that I suffered after a marathon, so I do have legitimate medical backing for this tip, as well as personal experience. After three days, the inflammation was significantly reduced. After three days, drop the dosage down to one or two Advil daily for another day or two, and then discontinue the Advil; it's not something to take daily for an extended period of time. If your injury doesn't seem to improve after three days, see a sports medicine professional.

99| Plantar Fasciitis Pain: A Runner's Bane

Plantar fasciitis is one of the most common injuries in runners. If you feel pain on the bottom of your foot at the front edge of your heel where it meets the arch, you may have plantar fasciitis. The fascia is a band of tissue that runs along the bottom of the foot. This band is flexible, and it flattens out and springs back with each step as you run. But if it is overstretched or if it rubs against something (like an ill-fitting shoe), it can become inflamed. Plantar fasciitis is caused by uneven weight distribution across that foot, which can arise from ill-fitting shoes or a lack of arch support. Running on concrete surfaces every day can aggravate the plantar fascia, too. Start by putting an ice pack on the sore spot for 10-15 minutes at a time a few times a day, especially after you have been running or walking. Review your shoes with a podiatrist. Your running shoe may have too much motion control and you may need a shoe with more flexibility, or vice versa. Plantar fasciitis will usually resolve within a few weeks if you address the cause. Some runners find that ultrasound treatment relieves plantar fasciitis, but it's important to find the cause of the problem and solve it to prevent chronic pain.

100| Prevention Is The Best Medicine For Marathon Training Injuries

Ideally, runners can build up their mileage and train for a marathon with no injuries. In reality, injuries happen, even to the most careful and well-conditioned runners. But you can reduce your risk of injury and reduce the severity of the injury with some preventive tips:

- Check your shoes (and orthotics): Don't train in worn-out shoes. Be sure to replace your shoes after 300-500 miles, depending on when you notice significant wear or any foot or leg pain. Even if you think that your shoes look and feel great, retire them at 500 miles. When you try on a new pair, you'll notice the difference. Many knee, hip, and back problems (as well as foot problems) are caused by poor foot alignment, which can occur when your shoes are worn out or because you need orthotics.
- Cross train: See the section on cross training tips for ways to keep your muscles strong and balanced.
- Rest: Don't forget to factor in a rest day each week so your muscles and joints can to recover from your tough training days.

101| Sports Massage

Whether you are a beginner or a seasoned marathoner, your body is adjusting to more stress of a different type than it has experienced before. A sports massage isn't medically necessary, but your muscles will thank you, and you may be preventing injuries by promoting circulation and reducing stiffness during your training. Also, sports massage can be helpful when you are returning to running after an injury. Any injury causes scar tissue to form, which makes the injured area less flexible. Massaging that area breaks up some of the scar tissue and promotes circulation, which promotes healing. Some insurance companies will cover sports massage or reimburse you if you have a flexible spending account, so investigate. Ask a fellow runner or a sports medicine professional to recommend a massage therapist who has had experience with athletes. A one-hour massage ranges from $60-$80, depending on where you live. Some therapists will do half-hour sessions that focus only on the legs, but I recommend a full-body massage a day or two before the marathon. Your upper body gets tight when you run, too, and why not give your muscles every advantage?

More Titles in the LifeTips Book Series

101 Green Travel Tips
by Linda Handiak

101 Entrepreneur Tips
by Susan Payton

101 Health Insurance Tips
by Michelle Katz

Printed in the United States
77485LV00001B/348